LITTLE BOOK OF

COARSE
FISHING

WITH **MATT HAYES**

LITTLE BOOK OF
COARSE
FISHING
WITH MATT HAYES

First published in the UK in 2013

© Demand Media Limited 2014

www.demand-media.co.uk

Printed and bound in Europe

ISBN 978-1-909217-58-4

CONTENTS

INTRODUCTION

Welcome to my guide to coarse fishing, and may it help in your quest to be a better angler. Whether you're a rank beginner, or someone looking to brush up on your skills, I hope they'll be something in this book to help you on your way.

I was very lucky – when I started fishing my father was on hand to show me the ropes. But others aren't so fortunate – and this is where books like this come in.

I've drawn on my 40-odd years as an angler to put this guide together and while it's difficult to condense four decades of knowledge into 128-pages, I am delighted with the outcome.

There are five key chapters; Choose the Right Tackle, Understanding Bait, Species Guide, Skills School and Fish Habitat. Each one is clear, concise and

written in 'angler's speak' – in other words, not bogged down by long-winded jargon!

The angling world is a large one that encompasses numerous disciplines. There are sea anglers who target the planet's oceans for huge sport fish and there are those who prefer trout and salmon, known as game anglers. But it's coarse fisherman who are found in the greatest numbers. And it's right here in the UK where the targeting of freshwater species like carp, roach, pike, tench, bream is at its popular.

The art of fishing can, of course, be traced back to the beginning of time when our ancestors would attempt to catch food for the table. But in time, as we evolved into a more civilised race, that basic need to survive has been

ABOVE Basking in the sun with this stunning carp

LEFT Morning breaks after a night of carp fishing

replaced by a desire to pit our wits against a wild, unpredictable, creature in the name of sport. Indeed, such is angling's draw that it has become the most popular participant past-time in the UK, with some two million anglers taking to the bank every weekend.

I am often asked what species and approach I enjoy the most. And I don't mind admitting that I probably give a different answer every time!

Why? The honest truth is that one week I can be enjoying fishing the float for tench, while the next I'm completely immersed in trying to outwit perch on lures.

And that, I think, is the real beauty of coarse fishing. It's hugely diverse, with so many different species to target, on so many different waters and different methods, that it's almost impossible to get bored.

What I've concluded after 40-odd years of being an angler is that we are extremely lucky. Not only do we get to enjoy the thrill of the chase and then –

LEFT A chub like this makes braving the cold worth while

FAR LEFT And the battle is won!

hopefully! – the adrenaline-rush of the battle, we do so against the backdrop of the great British countryside.

We're around for the golden dawns, the picture-postcard sunsets and the magical moments when we've been sat on the bankside long enough to blend in with the resident wildlife and become part of our surroundings.

Fishing, for me, has always been much more than about catching fish. It's been about the challenge, the anticipation, the unknown. It's been about getting away from the day-to-day routine of life and escaping into the great outdoors where a day can pass without ever seeing another human-being. I suppose, ultimately, it's been about recapturing that child-like thrill I experienced when I caught my first fish all those years ago.

So, enjoy the book. And I hope it helps on your angling journey.

Tight lines,

Matt Hayes

CHAPTER I

CHOOSE THE RIGHT TACKLE

Enter any tackle shop and you'll see a vast array of kit, from rods to reels, poles to seatboxes and everything else in between. To put it bluntly, it can be bewildering! So here's a run-down of the essential gear you'll need to get fishing, starting with rods.

RODS...

Fishing rods have come a long way from the time when a piece of garden cane or even a discarded tank aerial were used for the task. Most modern rods are made from carbon fibre, a material which is both light and flexible, although cheaper versions are constructed from fibreglass, which tends to make the rod heavier.

Here are the six main types of fishing rod:

FLOAT ROD

The most common type of rod is a float rod. Designed for use with floats, like wagglers and stick floats, a typical float rod is around 13ft long and comes in three sections. They are made longer to allow better control of a float. The general action of a float rod is 'all through,' meaning that when bent, it arcs all the way down the rod. This action suits the use of light line, small hooks and small fish.

LEGER ROD

Leger rods are designed for use with either bombs or swimfeeders and are a little stronger than float rods and also shorter, usually averaging around 11ft. The most popular style are quivertip

LEFT Quivertip fishing for bream

BELOW Float rod

RIGHT Carp rod

rods. These come with a built in quiver-tip – a very sensitive tip at the end of the rod that is normally brightly coloured. This is used for bite detection. Rods like this also have a 'through' action and are designed for relatively light lines and small to average-sized fish.

SPECIALIST ROD

Specialist rods are the preserve of the angler who wishes to target bigger fish, such as chub, barbel and tench. As big fish are the target, specialist rods pack plenty of power and typically have a test curve of between 1lb 8oz and 2lb. A test curve is determined by the weight needed to make a rod bend to its maximum and the larger the target of fish, the higher the test curve should be.

CARP ROD

Carp rods can be real brutes with test curves of 3lb but a typical example is around 2lb 8oz. This power is needed to cast heavy leger weights, as well as playing fish in excess of 20lb. Carp rods are two piece tools and have fewer rings than float and leger rods. A typical length is around 12ft.

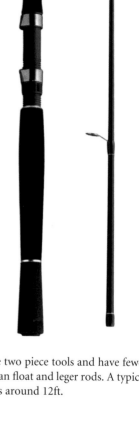

ABOVE Feeder rod

PIKE ROD

Like carp rods, pike rods are heavy duty tools designed for casting big baits long distances but they must also be forgiving to prevent hook pulls. For occasional pike fishing a carp rod would suffice but if you're serious about your piking, invest in one specifically designed for the job. Again they come in two sections and can boast a test curve of up to 3lb 8oz.

SPINNING RODS

These are probably the shortest rods on the market, with 8ft or 9ft the average length. The key to a good spinning rod is weight, because the angler can spend hours casting and retrieving a lure. Designed for hard-fighting predators like pike, they are built with plenty of power.

REELS...

" *The fishing reel is an essential piece of kit and it comes in four basic designs – the fixed spool, for general use, closed face, for match and river fishing, freespool, for big fish and a centrepin, the preferred option for river specialists.* "

FIXED SPOOL REEL

These are the most common reel on the market and the easiest to operate.

The basic design consists of a strong wire arm, known as the bail arm, that can be folded back across the spool to free the line from the spool for casting.

Once the cast is complete, a simple turn of the reel handle re-engages the arm, bringing it back across and trapping the line back on the spool.

Fixed spool reels also feature an anti-reverse lever that allows the spool to rotate without opening the bail arm – something that is important when playing fish. They also come with an adjustable drag (found either on the spool or on the back of reel) that also allows line to be released on demand.

CLOSED FACE REELS

One of the biggest problems with fixed spool reels is that the spool is open to the elements, especially the wind, which can create tangles.

The closed face reel eliminates this. Basically the spool's bail arm is replaced with a removable metal cover from which the line exits via a slot. The line is held in place by a pin that retracts inside the spool when a button on the front of the reel is pressed. This allows the angler to cast.

LEFT Fixed spool reel (see diagram on page 15)

However, the one down side of closed face reels is that there is no drag facility and so giving line to running fish is difficult.

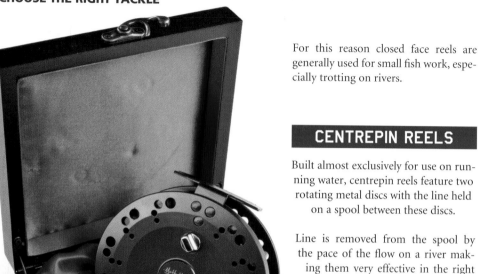

For this reason closed face reels are generally used for small fish work, especially trotting on rivers.

CENTREPIN REELS

Built almost exclusively for use on running water, centrepin reels feature two rotating metal discs with the line held on a spool between these discs.

Line is removed from the spool by the pace of the flow on a river making them very effective in the right hands.

However, the major drawback with a centrepin is in casting – it is not simply a case of removing a bail arm and allowing line to be freely released. Instead the angler must draw line from each of the rings before making an exaggerated sweep of the arm.

FREESPOOL REEL

These were originally designed by carp and big fish anglers in the 1970s. A freespool reel is normal fixed spool reel with a special facility that allows line to be released without opening the bail arm or fiddling with the drag.

When the bait is picked up and the fish and moves off, the line comes effortlessly from the spool. But once the rod is picked up, a simple turn on the reel disengages the freespool facility and reverts to behaving like a normal fixed spool reel.

They are commonly used by anglers legering for carp, pike, bream, barbel and tench.

FAR LEFT
Centrepin reel

WORKINGS OF A FIXED SPOOL REEL

1 Pick up or bail
2 Reel seat
3 Reel foot
4 Handle
5 Support arm
6 Anti-reverse lever
7 Skirted spool
8 Fishing line
9 Drag adjustment knob

POLES...

❝ Pole fishing might look simple, but there is more to it than simply attaching line to the end of a reel-less long rod! ❞

Like rods, poles are made with a number of materials but carbon fibre is by far the best, being light and strong. Some are constructed from a blend of fibreglass and carbon and these tend to be cheaper.

Poles are generally much longer than rods, with some up to 18 metres, although most tend to be around 11 metres and are made up of separate sections, normally in one metre lengths.

The tip sections of almost all poles contain elastic. This is tied directly to the line and acts as an absorber when the fish runs. Without it either the line

or pole would snap. Elastic comes in different strengths depending on the size of fish in question.

ROACH POLE

Roach poles are suited to traditional small fish angling on rivers, canals and lakes for species like roach and bream. They are light, fine pieces of tackle and feature flexible tips that are suited to elastics up to a Number 8 grade.

They, and most other poles on the market, are 'take apart', which means that

they can be broken down from their full length and fished at different lengths.

fish well into double figures.

CARP POLE

Carp poles are powerful tools yet, thanks to their carbon construction, are incredibly light and capable of landing

The extra strength comes from the thickness of the walls of the pole – they are reinforced to guard against breakages.

They also boast a stiffer tip, which allows the use of stronger elastics between Number 12 and 16.

MARGIN POLE

This type of pole is for specialist use when carp into double-figures are the target and its name gives away its purpose – for catching in the margins of a lake.

Shorter than a carp pole (averaging seven metres), margin poles are incredibly strong and very difficult to break.

The downside of this strength is weight but most margin fishing is only done at around four metres range so this isn't considered a problem.

WHIP

The preserve of the small fish angler, whips are unbeatable for catching nets of little fish like bleak, roach and gudgeon at speed on venues like canals and rivers and are therefore a specialised tool.

Typically measuring five metres in length, whips are like poles but are built without the elastic system. This is replaced instead with an extremely flexible solid carbon flicktip that acts as a shock absorber.

ELASTIC

Choose the right one...

Elastics come in different 'grades' and should be matched against the species the anglers wishes to catch. Here's a quick reference to choosing the right elastic.

NUMBER 1 – 6
ideal for small roach and perch when using a roach pole.

NUMBER 7 – 10
perfect for bream and tench on a carp pole.

NUMBER 11 – 15
spot on for carp to 8lb with a strong carp pole.

NUMBER 15 – 20
designed specifically for carp up to 15lb and best used with a margin pole.

RIG ESSENTIALS...

> *After you've bought your rod, reel or pole, you'll need a variety of other items before you can start fishing.*

HOOKS

Hooks come in different sizes, strengths and weights, depending on the type of metal they're made from.

RIGHT Barbed hooks

They range in size from a 2, which is the biggest, to a 26, which is the smallest.

Hooks come either barbed or barbless. The latter make unhooking easier and on many fisheries they are insisted upon.

You can either by hooks with an eye for attaching the line, or with a spade end.

Spade ends require line to be whipped on and are best bought ready-tied with hooklengths attached.

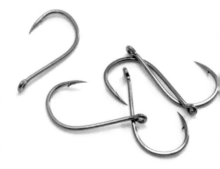

SHOT

Shot is normally used to provide casting weight when floatfishing and ranges in size from the largest at SSG rating to a tiny No 13 for delicate pole rigs.

RIGHT Monofilament is the most popular choice when it comes to mainline

Literally speaking, shot is a ball of metal with a split cut into it. Line is then placed in this split and the two halves pressed together to lock it in place.

BELOW Shot in various sizes

When locked correctly you will then be able to slide it up and down the line easily without casing damage.

LINE

Fishing line is made from monofilament – a fine, clear and supple material that ranges in strength and thickness.

It is rated in either pound or kilo divisions, ranging from very thin 1lb breaking strain to a heavy 20lb strength.

As well as mainline, you can also buy hooklength material. This is favoured by matchmen and is a short piece of monofilament, of lesser breaking strain, with a hook attached. This helps get more bites from shy-biting fish.

SWIMFEEDERS

Designed for introducing bait into tight patches around your hookbait, feeders come in three basic models, 'open end', 'blockend' or 'method.' These are explained in detail in 'Skills School – How to use a leger rig' on page 104-105.

LEGER WEIGHTS

Also known as bombs, legers are pear-shaped leads used as casting weight.

They are designed to keep a bait static on the bottom and are generally used by anglers who want to get a bait further out than a float will cast or are fishing

for long periods of time.

For a detailed breakdown of the type of leger weights available, turn to 'Skills School – How to use a leger rig' on page 104-105.

FLOATS

A float is a length of material, generally peacock quill, plastic or balsa wood, designed for use as a bite indicator and is a far more visual way of fishing than using a swimfeeder or leger weight.

There are four basic designs - straight waggler, insert waggler, bodied waggler and stick float and these are explained in detail in 'Skills School - How to shot a float' on page 102-103.

BOTTOM LEFT Leger weights come in various shapes and sizes

BELOW Selection of floats

KEY ITEMS...

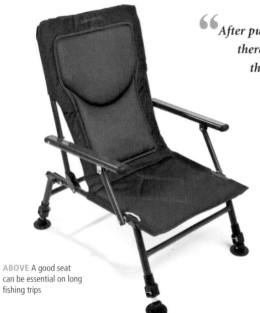

> *After purchasing tackle essentials, there are several other items that you can buy that will make your fishing life more comfortable.*

ABOVE A good seat can be essential on long fishing trips

CHAIRS

For some anglers a seatbox is just too unwieldy and not comfortable enough for long trips.

In this situation, custom-made collapsible chairs fit the bill perfectly. Most are made from strong, lightweight metals and can be easily carried around.

ROD RESTS

You don't need a rod rest to go fishing but you'll hit more bites by having one.

Rod rests are usually a plastic v-shaped rest that screws into separate metal stick, known as a bankstick. The rod rest is then situated directly in front of you, allowing you to place it in the rest, keeping the butt on your knee.

ROD PODS

The big fish angler's version of the rod rest, pods also overcome the problem of hard ground such as concrete and sun-backed mud.

A pod is a collapsible metal contraption that allows you to fish with up top three rods, boasting rests at either end for the rods to sit snugly on. They also come with special attachments to allow the use of bite alarms and bobbins.

ABOVE A rod pod

FORCEPS

For bigger fish a discorger is often not enough for unhooking – only forceps will do. These resemble surgical forceps and are metal scissors with blunt ends. These ends are used to grip the hook shank and safely the pull the hook out.

BITE ALARMS

These are electronic alarms, popular with carp, pike and big fish anglers.

They sit on a bankstick under the rod, usually between the handle and the first rod ring. The line running off the reel sits on top of a small free-running wheel within the alarm and as the line is pulled by a fish, the wheel spins and the alarm sounds.

FISHING UMBRELLA

Normally green, better umbrellas are made from a thick nylon material that is coated in a water repellent substance.

They also feature a strong pointed pole that should be stuck into the ground to stop the umbrella blowing away. Most are at least 42 inches across.

POLAROID GLASSES

The glare from sun shining onto the water can render vision almost down to

nil but Polaroid glasses help cut out this glare and are a useful piece of kit.

They are particularly popular amongst specimen hunters and river anglers especially.

WEIGHING SCALES

It pays to carry a set of scales in your carryall as you never know when that big fish will crop up.

You can buy purpose-made weighing scales from the tackle shop and they range in price from the inexpensive to expensive.

BOBBIN

If you can't afford a bite alarm, or you are only fishing for a short period, then a bobbin will tell you if you have a bite when legering.

It simply clips on the line between the reel and the first rod ring and when a fish takes the bait, it lifts up or drops down.

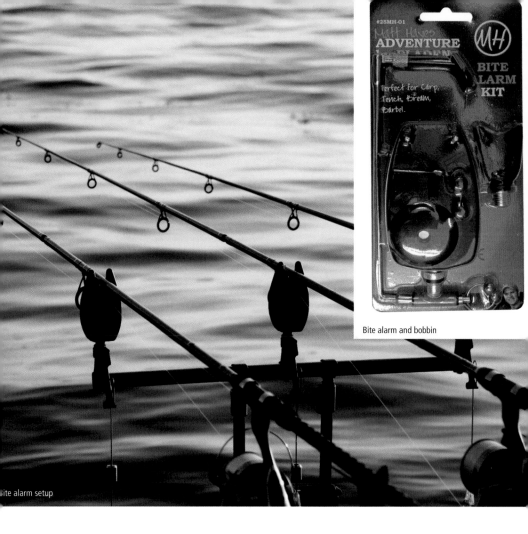

#25MH-01

Matt Hayes
ADVENTURE

BITE ALARM KIT

Perfect for carp, tench, bream, barbel.

Bite alarm and bobbin

Bite alarm setup

EXTRA TACKLE...

“ Together with line, shot and hooks, there are several other items of tackle you'll need to get the most from your day on the bank. ”

TACKLE BOXES

Tackle boxes are essential for keeping items like floats, hooks and shot safe and secure. Made of toughened plastic, they come in a variety of sizes but whichever one you choose, it will almost certainly feature separate compartments for each item of tackle.

KEEPNETS

Keepnets are used by match anglers for retaining their catch until the end

ABOVE Tackle boxes in various shapes and sizes

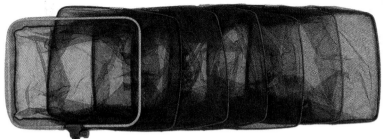

LEFT Keepnet

BELOW Triangular landing net and spoon shaped shallow net

if the contest. However, they are also popular in the pleasure angling fraternity, especially for those who like to see what they've caught at the end of the day. Modern keepenets average around 12ft long and are made with supersoft, knotless material to prevent damage to the fish.

LANDING NETS

Made of similar material to keepnets, landing nets vary greatly in size depending on what you're fishing for, from massive nets for big carp to tiny versions for roach on canals.

Deep triangular designs are favoured for big fish while match and pleasure anglers prefer a spoon-shaped shallow net.

BAIT BOXES

Purpose-made bait boxes are essential for retaining things like maggots, casters, worms and sweetcorn.

Made from plastic, they have secure lids with tiny holes in them that allow living bait to breathe – but not escape.

BELOW Bait boxes

LUGGAGE

While not essential, fishing luggage makes transferring your tackle to the bankside a whole lot easier. Modern luggage is light, strong, waterproof and capable of carrying everything you need for a day's fishing.

Rod holdalls will not only carry rods, they will also hold banksticks, umbrellas and poles. While a carryall will take tackle and bait boxes, together with nets and reels.

DISCORGERS

Another cheap and small item of tackle that no beginner should leave home without.

A discorger is simply a small plastic rod that enables the angler to safely unhook a fish that is not hooked in the lip, but deeper in the mouth.

SEAT BOXES

A good seatbox is capable of doing two things – providing something to sit on and allowing room for storage.

More advanced boxes boast drawers and trays to stash hooks, line, floats, pole rigs and feeders with a deep bottom base for larger items like reels. They also have adjustable legs and footplates for added comfort.

PLUMMETS

A plummet is a small and cheap item of tackle – but one that's absolutely vital. Essentially a piece of lead, it is attached to the hook when float fishing to enable the angler to determine how deep the water is.

CATAPULTS

If you want to feed your swim accurately, a catapult is also on the 'must have' list. Feeding by hand is fine if you are only fishing a few metres out, but if

you need to get bait out any further, a 'catty' is vital.

For loosefeeding baits like maggot, hemp and pellet a small match-style catapult is perfect whereas bigger stuff like boilies, or even balls of groundbait, require a more powerful model.

ABOVE A modern seatbox design

CHAPTER 2

UNDERSTANDING BAIT

Just because pellets and boilies dominate today's fishing, it's definitely worth incorporating more traditional baits into your armoury, many still have the same pulling powers.

MAGGOTS
AND CASTERS...

There's a reason why maggots and casters are so popular – they're among the best fish-catchers of the lot!

Virtually every species will eat maggots and although they are considered predominantly a small-fish bait, the likes of carp and tench will happily eat them, too.

Casters, meanwhile, are often capable of sorting out the bigger fish in a shoal. For example, you can be catching small roach in the 2oz bracket when a change to caster will suddenly produce a better stamp.

The simple maggot is the larvae of the blow fly and although they can be bred at home, it's far more convenient to buy them from tackle shops. They should be stored in a fridge to keep them fresh.

The next stage of the maggot's metamorphosis before it becomes a fly is when it turns into a caster. Casters are initially almost white in colouration when they first turn but gradually darken as they become older. They don't last long – no more than a few days – before they turn into flies. They should also be stored in a fridge.

ABOVE Maggots are an all-time favourite bait

WHAT COLOUR?

In their natural state maggots are white but they can also be bought in variety of colours. Red tends to be the most popular. Why this is the case is open to speculation, but some believe it's because they resemble bloodworm – which are the natural diet of most species. Bronze is another colour that has traditionally performed well, especially with roach. If you prefer something a bit different, you can buy green, blue or even fluro coloured maggots – all of which will catch fish on their day.

OTHER VARIETIES OF MAGGOT

As well as the standard maggot, you can also use pinkies and squats.

RIGHT Casters

FAR RIGHT Bronze maggots

Pinkies are the larvae of greenbottle flies and are smaller in size. As the name suggests, they are largely pink but are also available in alternative colours. They tend to be used in winter, when the fishing is hard, and are often the favourite of the matchman.

Squatts are even smaller than pinkies and are usually added to groundbait when species like bream are the target.

CASTERS

While it's possible to produce your own casters (you essentially let your maggots turn and remove the casters at intervals) it's far more convenient to buy them from a tackle shop. Although more expensive than maggots, they are a great change bait from maggots and, as mentioned earlier, will often catch a better quality fish. Casters should be kept in a fridge and once on the bank are best stored in a bait box with a covering of water. This will prevent them from drying out.

PUTTING MAGGOTS AND CASTERS ON THE HOOK

Maggots and casters are both brilliant baits but they will be rendered useless if they aren't hooked correctly. When it comes to maggots, you should gently squeeze the grub until a small tuft appears at the blunt end. This is where you should enter the hookpoint. Casters require an equally delicate approach. You can either nick through the blunt end of bury the hook inside. Either way, it's vital the bait isn't smashed.

WHICH HOOK FOR WHICH BAIT?

It's absolutely crucial you match the correct hook with the correct bait. If you don't, you'll either ruin your presentation or miss crucial bites.

Here's a rough guide to what you should be using...

Size 24	Single squatt
Size 22	Single pinkie
Size 20	Single maggot/breadpunch/hemp
Size 18	Double maggot
Size 16	Redworm/triple maggot
Size 14	Brandling worm/grain of sweetcorn
Size 12	Breadflake/half a lobworm
Size 10	Mini boilie
Size 8	Cheesepaste/breadflake/small livebait
Size 6	Lobworm/boilie/Cheesepaste
Size 4	Two lobworms
Size 2	Slug

BOILIES...

> *Go back 30 years, and boilies were unheard of. Fast-forward to the modern era and no self-respecting big fish angler would ever leave home without them!*

Carp, in particular, absolutely love boilies, and on some waters they are rarely caught on anything else.

SO WHAT ARE THEY?

These proven fish-catchers, which come in many different sizes from a tiny 8mm to a giant 40mm, are also available in a huge range of colours and flavours, too.

They are specially formulated with a mixture of ground bird seeds, fishmeal and sometimes milk proteins as the primary, bulk ingredients.

These powdered ingredients are mixed with different flavours and the resulting mix is then bound with eggs and rolled into baits of varying sizes and boiled – hence the name 'boilie' - to give them a hardened outer layer.

ABOVE Carp caught on a boilie

referred to as HNV baits. And it's this nutritional value that makes them so attractive to fish.

On waters where they are introduced in numbers, they become the chief source of food - and because of the quality of ingredients, that means the species that eat them put on weight quickly. They'll also ignore other baits in their search for boilies.

FULL OF FLAVOUR

First developed for use in carp fishing in the 1970s, boilies have a high nutritional value and, as such, were once

FROZEN OR FRESH?

Boilies can be made from scratch, indeed experienced carp anglers like to add their own 'special' ingredients when making their own. However, so many bait companies make their own, that it's far less hassle (and probably cheaper, too) to buy them ready-rolled.

The choice then is whether to buy freezer baits or shelf-life boilies. The former are arguably better, because they contain 'active' ingredients that require the bait to be kept in the freezer. Once removed, they will sour over a period of a few days.

Shelf-life boilies are more practical because they contain preservatives that enable them to last for a much longer period of time.

BAITS FOR SPECIMEN FISH

Boilies are so named because they are boiled to give them a hard outer skin. This makes them more resistant to the attentions of smaller fish and enables the angler to use them safe in the knowledge only bigger specimens will be able to pick them up.

Being durable, they can also be left in the water for long periods of time without the need to recast.

BELOW Boilies in a variety of colours

ALL SHAPES, SIZES AND COLOURS

The smallest boilies you can buy are tiny 8mm ones (ideal for bigger roach and bream), while the biggest can proper gob-stoppers at 40mm (generally used for catfish or huge carp)! More common sizes are 12mm, 14mm and 16mm.

When it comes to colour, the choice is yours! You can opt for dullish reds or browns, or fluro yellows, pinks and greens. Experiment to see what works on your venue.

BUOYANT BOILIES

The standard boilie is a 'bottom bait' – and this means it sits on the lake or river bed. But you can buy pop-ups, too. These are buoyant boilies that will sit just off the bed of the lake making them easier for the fish to find and take. Pop-ups can be used in various situations, but normally where there is weed or silt present.

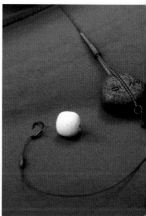

THE BEST PRESENTATION

A hair-rig is undoubtedly the best, and most natural, way to present a boilie. The 'hair' is essentially an extension of the hooklength that sits, with a small loop at the end, underneath the hook. The boilie is then threaded up the hair and kept in place with a stop.

The end result is a bait that is clear of the hook – and that means it will behave as naturally as it would if it were a free offering.

TOP LEFT Two hair-rigged boilies

TOP RIGHT Boilie on a carp rig

BREAD...

Versatile, readily available and cheap, bread is one of the all-time great fishing baits.

It can be fished under a float – either with rod and line or with a pole – in conjunction with a feeder or lead, or simply by itself on the hook or as feed. What's more, aside from predators, every other coarse fish will eat it!

Perhaps the best way of looking at the uses for bread is to breakdown how it can be applied, both as hookbait and feed.

BREADPUNCH

Very much a small-fish bait, and one associated with the winter months, breadpunch involves using small punches to remove small discs from the bread.

A sliced loaf is essential and the bread must be fresh and tacky for it work at its best. A slice is simply removed from the loaf, and then placed on a hard surface. A punch size is then chosen (these are available in sizes that remove discs from a few millimetres in width to close around 1cm) and then pushed into the bread. The resulting disc is then used on the hook. Breadpunch is at its most effective when presented under a pole float.

BREADFLAKE

Breadflake is the name given to bread that is removed from the soft inner of the loaf and the mounted on the hook. You can use any size you wish – from a small 'pinch' that would be suitable for trotting for roach, to a big 50p-sized bait that might be picked up by a big carp.

BELOW Breadflake on hook

Once taken from the loaf, the bread is then folded and pinched around the shank of the hook, with the end left invitingly fluffy. Care should be taken not to mask the hookpoint, which should always be left exposed.

BREAD CRUST

The crust of the bread is buoyant – and that makes it a great surface bait for species like carp.

Simply tear off a chunk, attach to a suitable sized hook – say a 6 – and cast out. But crust isn't just a big carp bait. Chub and rudd will also take it, albeit in smaller sizes.

You can also try and anchor pieces off the bottom – experiment in distance to see what works on any given day.

LIQUIDISED

Liquidised bread is superb at attracting fish into the swim without filling them up. Small balls can be used when float-fishing for species like chub and roach, or it can be put through a feeder when targeting the same fish.

Prepare bread by removing the crusts from sliced bread and then introducing to a blender.

MASH

Soaking and working stale loaves through your fingers will create mash.

When introduced, mash feeds a swim with lots of different sized pieces of waterlogged bread together with an attractive milky cloud effect.

At its best as a winter chub attractor.

Breadflake and maggot combination

PELLETS, PASTE AND LUNCHEON MEAT...

It always pays to carry a range of hookbaits and although maggots, casters, worms and bread might be traditional favourites, the advent of commercial, artificially-stocked, waters has led to a rise in three others, too. Let's take a look at pellets, paste and luncheon meat.

PELLETS

Largely made up of fishmeals and fish oils, they come in a variety of sizes from 4mm to 20mm-plus. Halibut, carp and trout pellets are the most common type. Here are the most common:

I. HALIBUT PELLETS

High in oil and full of proteins and nutrients, halibuts come in a range of sizes. Perhaps most effective as a bigger bait, they can be drilled and hair-rigged for species like barbel, carp and catfish.

2. TROUT PELLETS

Another pellet with a high oil – and protein – content. Great as feed in the summer when the oil will escape and leak into the water.

3. CARP PELLETS

A great option for feed on venues where trout and halibut pellets aren't allowed.

Some fisheries impose a ban because of the oil content, which can damage the fish if used in vast quantities. Carp pellets are based on harmless vegetable proteins and break down quickly.

4. SOFT HOOKERS

Pellets are naturally too hard to put directly on the hook but one way around this is to buy specifically prepared 'hookers'. These are often flavoured and come in small, re-sealable, pots.

5. EXPANDERS

These are hard but buoyant pellets that have to be prepared before use. Either soak in water, or use purpose-designed pellet pump, to produce a 'spongey' pellet that leaks of flavour but is also hook friendly.

ABOVE Expander pellets

LEFT Classic carp pellets and a PVA bag with a pellet on the hook

6. FLAVOURED PELLETS

These are essentially halibut or carp pellets that have been coloured and flavoured for use as predominantly as feed. For example, you can buy a pellet in exactly the same flavour as your boilies – and that can be a great edge.

These can also be used in the hook with the help of a pellet band – a piece of elastic that fits around the pellet then slips on the hook.

LUNCHEON MEAT

Luncheon meat is a superb bait for all coarse fish, especially barbel, chub, carp, tench and bream.

What's more, it's incredibly easy to use. Simply open the tin, take out the meat and cut it to the size required.

A species like carp will happily take a matchbox-sized cube, whereas tench may want something smaller. For the bigger pieces, a hair-rig provides the best presentation.

BOOST MEAT WITH FLAVOUR

While meat straight from the tin is excellent, a little flavour can really give it the edge. This can be done one of two ways. Either cut it into bait-size pieces and fry with chilli powder, or place the pieces into an air-tight container with your chosen flavour and freeze. When defrosted, the flavour will be drawn into the meat.

PASTES

Paste can either be made at home, or bought ready-to-use from tackle shops. The ingredients are often the same as those included in boilies but instead of being rolled into balls and boiled, the paste is broken off and moulded around the hook.

Softer paste is the better paste – basically because it will leak off more enticing flavour into the water. However, if it's soft, it won't stay on the hook very well. That means a pole is the best way of presenting it. The paste lasts for a few

minutes before it must be replaced – the bonus being you are consistently feeding the swim.

TRADITIONAL FAVOURITES

Bread paste is perhaps the most popular of the home-made pastes, and can be made by kneading slightly stale bread in the hands while slowly adding water until the right consistency is reached.

The other popular paste is cheesepaste. To make it add either stale bread and grated cheese together or mix of Danish Blue and fresh shortcrust pastry. Try adding margarine to make both softer if needed.

ABOVE Cheese paste

LEFT TOP Luncheon meat cubes

LEFT BOTTOM A barbel caught on luncheon meat

WORMS AND OTHER NATURAL BAITS...

"*While the tackle shop is full of all manner of different baits, there are some that are completely free – if you put in a little effort to collect them.*"

WORMS

Worms are surely the most popular – and effective – of these natural options. Loved by fish of all species, they can be absolutely deadly – as long as you know which type of worm to use…

LOBWORMS

The 'lobby' is the biggest of the three earthworms that are commonly used by anglers. You can find them in your back garden where they can be dug or collected from a wet lawn after dark. They are then best stored in damp newspaper or moss. The lobworm is immediately recognisable, largely because it is so much larger than its cousins. It has a reddish brown colour with a tail slightly fatter and broader than the rest of its body. A whole lob is a fantastic perch bait, but will equally be devoured by the likes of tench and carp, too.

BRANDLINGS

Found in manure and compost heaps,

ABOVE Lobworms

brandlings generally congregate in vast numbers so collecting them is easy. They are considerably smaller than lobworms and only grow to about four inches in length. They are also a different colour, being red in appearance with a soft skin that's lined with a series of yellow rings. Single brandlings are great for perch, roach and rudd, while bunches are good for tench and bream.

REDWORMS

Small, lively and easy to find (compost heaps are again the place to look) redworms are a superb fish-catcher They share similarities with the brandling but are without yellow hoops so are easy enough to tell apart. They can be fished individually for small species like perch, roach, skimmer bream and rudd, or in bunches for bigger bream and tench.

BLOODWORM

The bloodworm is perhaps the finest fish-catcher of them all – mainly because it forms the staple diet of nearly every species that swims. The 'little red men' as they are sometimes referred to, are water-based and live in silt beds. They are very small – a few millimetres in length – and brilliant red in colouration. Although superb at catching fish, they are extremely difficult to collect and as such, they are expensive to buy. They are also very difficult to handle and tend to be only used by matchmen.

TRY CHOPPED WORM

If you are fishing worm on the hook, the best thing to use with it is chopped worm. This can be introduced as loosefeed or mixed in groundbait but either way it's a hugely effective way of enticing fish into the swim without filling them up. Simply take a handful of worms, place in a bait tub, and then use a pair of scissors (these can be bought multi-bladed) to chop them into tiny pieces. The resulting 'mush' is a scent-laden bomb that perch, especially, absolutely love.

PUTTING WORMS ON THE HOOK

Worms are a brilliant bait – but they need to be mounted on the hook with care. There are three things to ensure:

1. The worm must be able to withstand the cast.

2. It must be free to wriggle is as natural a manner as possible.

3. The hook point is left free so a strike results in a hooked fish.

Small worms like brandlings and redworms can be hooked through the middle, but lobworms should be hooked cleanly through the thicker and darker coloured saddle. A good tip is to then put a maggot, or a thin sliver of elastic band, on the hook to prevent the worm from escaping. This is especially vital if you are using a barbless hook.

OTHER NATURALS

Here are a few less commonly used natural baits that are well worth a try...

PRAWNS

Carp, tench and perch love fresh prawns. Try dipping them in a bait glug for added attraction.

COCKLES

These are a great bait for tench – especially in summer. Fish them under a float in the margins.

SLUGS

Brilliant when freelined for chub, slugs can be collected from the garden and stored in a bait box. Mount on a size 2 or 4 hook.

SEEDS, PULSES AND NUTS...

" The most popular forms of seeds, nuts and pulses are hemp, sweetcorn, maize and tiger nuts... "

Also known as 'particles' - a term that refers to the fact they are usually very small - they and are mostly used in quantities during the summer to entice fish into the swim without filling them up.

SEEDS

HEMP

Possibly the finest attractor of them all, hemp is usually employed as a means of drawing fish into a swim rather than a hookbait.

With each seed being so small, fish can spend a long time in a peg searching and grubbing around – and that means more time for them to find your hookbait.

Perfect for big carp, tench and bream, it's loved by barbel and chub on rivers as well. Hemp is used as a hookbait for roach during the colder months when it is usually floatfished on light tackle and a small hook.

ABOVE Hemp and tares

RIGHT Hemp

PULSES

SWEETCORN

This is a real favourite with anglers, especially in summer, when it will catch almost all species.

It's great on the hook or for use as feed and is easy to acquire tinned or frozen. Corn also takes on colours and flavours well, a trick that can catch fish when they become wary of it in its plain, yellow form. Brilliant for tench, bream, chub and carp.

MAIZE

Maize is essentially giant sweetcorn and its attractiveness tends to be improved when it starts to ferment. It is mostly used by specialist anglers who wish to target big carp.

TARES

Originally used for feeding pigeons, these make excellent hookbaits for roach.

They are best fished on the hook when hemp is loosefed but remember, they need to be boiled prior to use.

NUTS

TIGER NUTS

with carp fishing and a tiger nut is an excellent hookbait for the species.
The attraction of nuts lie in their strong smell, which gets even stronger as they ferment, and their high oil content. Crushed or liquidised nuts also make a superb groundbait additive.

PEANUTS

These are another superb carp bait – but not the salted ones readily bought in supermarkets.

They should be boiled before and, like tiger nuts, are well worth adding

to groundbait when they have been crushed into small pieces.

PREPARE YOUR BAIT CORRECTLY

The most important thing to remember when using any of these baits, but especially the bigger pulses and all the nuts, is that they must be prepared correctly otherwise they can prove damaging to fish.

Seeds, pulses, grains and nuts must be first soaked and then boiled for long enough to ensure they have absorbed as much moisture as possible.

If fish eat baits that aren't properly cooked then they can continue to absorb water and swell in a fish's stomach thereby causing it potentially fatal harm.

Remember, most tackle shops sell cooked hempseed and nuts and the inexperienced angler should use these first.

LIVEBAITS, DEADBAITS AND LURES...

> *Species like pike, perch and zander are referred to as predators, which essentially means they live on a diet largely consisting of other fish. So the best way to target them is with livebaits, deadbaits and lures.*

LIVEBAITS

There are strict rules in place when it comes to livebaiting and some fisheries ban it completely so check before you even consider it.

If allowed, the fish to be used as bait must be caught from the venue you are fishing – transferring live fish between waters is strictly prohibited.

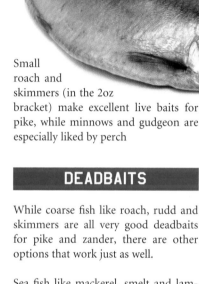

Small roach and skimmers (in the 2oz bracket) make excellent live baits for pike, while minnows and gudgeon are especially liked by perch

DEADBAITS

While coarse fish like roach, rudd and skimmers are all very good deadbaits for pike and zander, there are other options that work just as well.

Sea fish like mackerel, smelt and lamprey are all proven coarse-fish catchers. Let's have a look at each in detail…

MACKEREL

These are a highly successful bait for pike. They can be fished whole or in sections and are good for long range

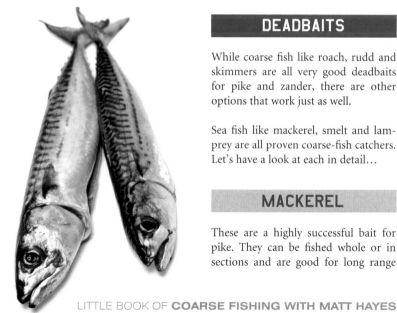

ABOVE Herring deadbait

LEFT Mackerel deadbait

casting because they are firm and stay on the hook.

They are an oily fish that leak off enticing juices underwater so a good trick is to cut them into sections before use.

SMELT

Smelt give off a really strong smell and their whiteish colour makes them very visible underwater. They are a favourite with pike and zander and are readily available from fishmongers.

LAMPREY

This is a form of eel that is best used when cut into sections. Again it gives off juices underwater which attract predatory fish like a magnet and pike, chub and catfish all love lamprey.

LURES

Lure fishing is becoming increasingly popular across Europe because it requires the minimum of tackle and allows the angler to be mobile.

Generally lures are designed to either mimic prey or encourage the fish to attack through their vivid colours and noise. They come in four basic patterns…

SPOONS

Spoons are bigger than spinners and generally do not have a separate spinning body, instead being made of a solid metal. They work visually, normally being silver or gold and can look dramatic when they catch the sun. Pike and perch fall to spoons.

SPINNERS

These are so called because they feature a blade that rotates. They attract fish because of their bright, shiny colour – and also by vibrating underwater. These vibrations alert the attention of predators. Perch are the main species that fall for this type of lure.

PLUGS

These are perhaps the most attractive of lures – and those that mostly resemble fish.

The factor that makes them so effective is they can be retrieved through the water at a specific depth which is determined by the plastic 'lip' they have at their 'nose'.

Again they come in a variety of colours and sizes and some even contain a rattle which encourage the fish to strike. Perch, pike, zander and chub will all be caught on plugs

JIGS

These are a relatively new invention and get their name from the way they move across the bottom when retrieved. They are made of rubber and have just a single hook which is weighted to reach the bottom. The large rubber 'dress' they boast provides brilliant visual stimulation and jigs are excellent lures for catching perch and pike.

CHAPTER 3

SPECIES GUIDE

Now you've learnt about what tackle you'll need and what bait to use, it's time to learn about the fish, where they live and how to catch them...

A shoal of roac

BARBEL...

IDENTITY

The barbel is a perfect river fish with its streamlined body shape. It has is a lean shape underslung mouth, which boasts four barbules – two small ones at the tip of the nose and two longer ones at the sides of the mouth. These feelers help locate food. It has bronze flanks, dark fins and a white underbelly and is known for its fighting qualities.

They can grown to more than 20lb (9k) in some European countries, but the average weight is more like 5lb (2.5k).

DISTRIBUTION

You'll find barbel in west and central Europe, including south east England, east to Russia and the Black Sea. Absent from Scotland and Ireland.

LOCATION

Barbel are very much a river fish but commercial fisheries do now stock them. They love fast water and often hang where the pace is so strong that silt cannot build up on the bottom, leaving clean gravel instead. Barbel love gravel! Weirs are another barbel hotspot because of the constant influx of fresh water.

It is over this clean gravel that barbel spawn in late Spring, vast numbers head to shallow areas where females create a small dent in the gravel to lay their which are then fertilised by the males.

DIET

If left to their own devices, barbel would munch on insect larvae, snails and freshwater mussels. They have also been known to eat small fish too, although this is less common.

Feeding times are dictated by the weather conditions. During the summer months, they will eat at dawn and dusk, with the first few hours of darkness a period being favoured. In winter, when the water is cold, they are less active but if the river is in flood, they have been known to feed heavily. Since the introduction of pellets into rivers by anglers, barbel appear to have flourished, packing on the pounds.

TACTICS

You can try float or leger, even fly, but in general bottom fishing is best. On small rivers, where it's possible to feed by hand or a bait-dropper, a straightforward leger weight is a very good approach. On bigger rivers, a feeder is the preferable option.

Barbel love hempseed and this is a great way of getting them into the swim and holding them there. Once occupied on these tiny grains, sweetcorn, luncheon meat or boilies work. In recent times, pellets have made an impact, both for a hookbait and in the feeder.

In winter, if the water is coloured due to flooding, use a smelly, oily bait like luncheon meat to attract their attention. Don't be scared to use a big lump. Barbel fight hard by using their shape in the fast water so stout tackle is needed. Think nothing of using 10lb mainline, more in snaggy venues.

They have four barbules around their mouths which are very sensitive and used for feeding.

Barbel have been artificially stocked into stillwaters but are normally found in rivers.

LEFT Landing a quality barbel

BELOW A great example of a big barbel

FACTFILE

The latin name for barbel is barbus barbus.

The can live for more than 15 years.

Barbel love to 'flank' – a term used to describe them twisting their bodies while they are feeding.

They love clean gravel because it provides a rich feeding ground.

FIVE BAITS TO TRY FOR BARBEL

BOILIES
PELLETS
SWEETCORN
LUNCHEON MEAT
PASTE

BREAM...

" *Bream are a shoal fish and love to graze over beds of food.* "

IDENTITY

Bream have deep, narrow bodies and it's this shape that has led anglers to call small fish 'skimmers' and bigger specimens, those over 3lb, 'slabs.' Younger fish tend to have a silver appearance, while older ones are a darker bronze.

DISTRIBUTION

Bream found all across England and most of Europe.

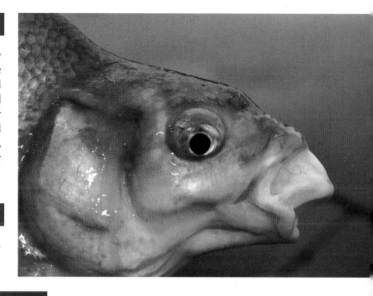

LOCATION

Bream are one of the most widespread of all coarse fish and live in a variety of different waters from lakes and gravel pits to drains, canals and rivers.

They move in vast shoals, sometimes hundreds strong, where they lazily graze over gravel and silt beds in search of food.

For the best chance of catching one, look to fish a lake or gravel pit.

The species loves wide open spaces where it can graze before moving on to another feeding area.

Bream aren't a marginal species and are found further out, normally around underwater features like gravel bars, depressions or plateaus.

ABOVE Close-up of a bream's mouth, perfect for feeding on bottom-dwelling insects and plant material

LEFT Example of a small bream

RIGHT Bream on net

They normally spawn at the end of May or early June, when the water temperature begins to warm up. Males are easy to recognise at this time because they grown hard spawning tubercles around their heads and bodies.

Each female lays as many as 400,000 eggs, of which only a fraction survive. A bream that weighs 7lb is thought to be around 10 years old.

DIET

They feed on a wide range of plant material, insect larvae and other bottom-dwelling insects.

TACTICS

A groundbait approach is best. Feed plenty of bait to keep the shoal in the area.

Sweetcorn, pellets, maggots, casters, worms and small boilies are all great baits for bream.

FACTFILE

The Latin name for bream is abramis brama.

They have a thick protective layer of slime over their bodies.

Bream live in huge shoals where they graze like cattle over gravel and silt beds.

They have very soft, small underslung mouths which project forwards when rooting for food.

Bream show themselves by rolling – normally at dawn or dusk.

The average bream lives to 15 years of age but can reach 20.

FIVE BAITS TO TRY FOR BREAM

MAGGOTS
CASTERS
WORMS
SWEETCORN
MINI-BOILIES

CARP...

> *Carp, both big and small, have become the UK's most popular fish.*

IDENTITY

Europe's most popular fish, the carp is loved for its size, its fighting ability and also because it's an extremely hardy species.

Let's look at the different types of carp you may catch:

Common carp - fully scaled and golden in appearance.

Mirror carp – covered with a random scattering of scales

Leather carp - smooth and scale-less.

There are also grass carp and crucian carp, but these are very different creatures in body shape, size and behaviour. Although commons, mirrors and leathers differ in appearance, they share the same broad, deep shape and general browny/yellow colourartion. They also have the same four barbules around their mouths, and these enable the carp to feel and taste food. Carp grow to huge sizes. Fish approaching 100lb have been caught on the Continent and while the

UK's biggest is under 70lb, fish of 20lb or more are caught on a regular basis.

DISTRIBUTION

Carp in their various guises can be found across Europe, except for Iceland. In the UK, largely thanks to the climate, the bigger specimens are found in the south.

LOCATION

Carp live in almost freshwater venues but lakes, gravel pits and ponds are

BELOW Always a pleasure catching a carp like this!

more likely destinations than fast-moving rivers.

Places that are rich in plant life, where they lazily root around the bottom in search of food, are favoured. When carp spawn depends on the temperature, but the water needs to be warm. May and June, therefore, is the most likely period.

The female lays over one million eggs among the weed in the shallows and when they hatch, the surviving fry rapidly become fish. Carp are a fast growing species and, in the right environment, will reach 2lb in a year.

DIET

Snails, bloodworms, mussels and anything else they can find in the mud on the bottom of the venue are on the menu for carp. They have large mouths and spend hours sucking and blowing out morsels of food, sending plumes of bubbles to the surface in the process.

While they are predominantly bottom feeders, they will also come to the surface and take small insects off the top. Carp are at their most active during the warmer summer months but they can still be caught in winter when cold snaps are broken by small rise in the temperature.

TACTICS

Whatever way you fish for carp, stout kit is required.

Floatfishing does work but most anglers tend to leger, primarily because bites are infrequent and often occur during darkness – and that renders a float uselss.

Target swims with trees, islands or underwater gravel bars because carp, like all fish, love to move around in these areas.

As mentioned, nightfall is perhaps the best time to catch carp although dawn and dusk are also excellent feeding spells.

For bait, go for something like boilies, pellets, paste, bread or sweetcorn. But if the fish are feeding on the surface, floating crust or a dog biscuit make a great alternative.

FACTFILE

The latin name for carp is cyprinus carpio.

Carp come in a several varieties including common, mirror and leather.

Carp can live to be more than 40 years old.

Although mostly found on the bottom, carp love to cruise around under the surface in the summer months where they eat insects from the surface.

Night-time is often the best time where carp are concerned.

FIVE BAITS TO TRY FOR CARP

BOILIES
SWEETCORN
DOG BISCUITS
BREAD
PELLETS

CHUB...

"Chub eat almost anything from small fish, insects and worms, to plankton."

IDENTITY

Big chub are easily recognisable by their brassy coloured flanks, orange anal fins and huge, white lips but smaller ones are often mistaken for dace.

The definitive way of being 100% sure is by checking the dorsal and anal fins. The chub has rounded, convex-shaped fins while the dace is concave.

Can grow close to 10lb in weigh but the average size is around 3lb

DISTRIBUTION

Throughout all of Europe except Iceland, Ireland, southern Spain and southern Italy.

LOCATION

Chub are caught from stillwaters (either escapees from rivers during flood conditions are specifically stocked) but they are normally found in running water. Look for the middle or lower reaches of a river where, as a shy, retiring fish, they love the cover of overhanging trees, weedbeds and undercut banks.

Stillwater chub tend to have a different shape to those that inhabit rivers. They are more barrel-shaped in appearance and less stream-lined.

DIET

Chub eat almost anything from small fish, insects and worms, to plankton. Although they don't have teeth in their mouth, they do have very powerful pharyngeal teeth at the back of their throat which are capable of crushing almost any food item.

TACTICS

Both floatfishing and legering will catch river-dwelling chub. If you prefer the former, then trotting a bait like maggots under a stickfloat is very effective.

Others prefer to cast a leger near to overhanging trees with something like

LEFT A great example of a chub in perfect condition

ABOVE Close-up of a chub

RIGHT Good size chub caught in running water

bread, boilies or cheesepaste on the hook. Remember, though, only use enough lead to hold bottom – chub can be extremely wary and will drop a bait if they feel resistance.

In summer, when the water is clear, it's possible to stalk fish by creeping up on them and then watching them take the bait.

Stillwater chub are traditionally harder to catch than those in running water. If you wish to fish for them try float-fished maggot but you'll need plenty of loosefeed to keep them interested. Alternatively, a bolt-rig set-up with a boilie as hookbait will work if you are after the biggest of specimens.

FIVE BAITS TO TRY FOR CHUB

SWEETCORN
BREAD
WORMS
CHEESEPASTE
BOILIES

PERCH...

"As predators, perch eat other fish, especially species like minnows, small roach and gudgeon."

IDENTITY

Surely the most handsome of all our coarse fish, the perch simply cannot be mistaken for any other species.

Its olive-green flanks are marked with up to seven black stripes and, when erect, its large, spiked dorsal fin is a striking sight. Incidentally, the points of this dorsal fin are sharp and require the angler to handle with caution. A firm, but not too tight, grip is needed when holding these fish.

The pectoral and anal fins are blood red in appearance but generally the perch is coloured to fit in with its environment. It's a predatory fish that likes to merge with the weeds and underwater debris it lurks in before striking at prey.

DISTRIBUTION

Despite suffering a set-back in the 1970s when disease wiped out a large proportion of the perch population, they have recovered very well and populate almost all venues throughout the UK.

LOCATION

Although they can be found in all manner of water courses, perch prefer lakes, ponds, slow-moving rivers, drains and canals.

Perch are sight-feeders so they thrive in clear water venues. This doesn't mean they don't live in muddier, carp-dominate commercials, just that they are much harder to catch.

This is a species that loves cover. Anywhere they can hide in readiness to pounce on prey fish, is a good place to find perch. Therefore, bridges, river and canal locks, overhanging trees and underwater tree roots are all superb areas to start.

Spawning occurs between March and June when the female lays up to 350,000 eggs.

DIET

As predators, perch eat other fish, especially species like minnows, small roach

LEFT A stunning example of a big perch showing the distinctive spiked dorsal fin

ABOVE A nice perch on a cold day

RIGHT TOP perch caught on a plug

RIGHT BOTTOM A big perch hooked on a lure

and gudgeon. Basically, anything they can find!

Interestingly, as crayfish have become more prevalent in the UK, especially in river networks, they have become part of the diet for perch. And in these venues, the many of the species have grown particularly large on the protein-rich crays.

Small perch will hunt in shoals, while bigger fish hunt in packs or three or four.

Although perch have been known to reach 8lb-plus on the Continent, the best in the UK is 6lb 4oz. Anything over 3lb is considered a real specimen.

TACTICS

Just like pike, perch respond well to live or deadbaits. Obviously as a smaller species, they require a smaller bait so go for something like a gudgeon, minnow or roach between 1oz and 2oz.

While deadbaiting does occasionally work, a live fish, presented beneath a float, is by far the most effective way of catching perch. However, check with the fishery first – some venues ban the practice. If it is allowed, you must catch your 'lives' from the water you intend to fish; transferring live fish is banned.

Another great bait for perch is lobworm. The best approach is to floatfish (perch hate resistance) and a lob presented over a bed of chopped worm can be devastating on the right day.

The last way of targeting big perch is to use artificals. Spinners, small plugs and small spoons all work, as do jigs and jellyworms.

With any of the above you are trying to convince the perch that your lure is a real fish so try and make it behave like one.

The great thing about lures are that

they enable the angler to cover a lot of ground and that can be crucial when hunting predators.

FACTFILE

The Latin name for perch is perca fluviatilis.

They are easy to spot by their spiny dorsal fin.

Female perch generally grow much bigger than males.

Perch are predatory and feed on other fish.

Clear water is vital to catching perch because they hunt by sight.

FIVE BAITS TO TRY FOR PERCH

WORMS
LIVE FISH
MAGGOTS
JIGS
SPINNERS

PIKE...

A lean body capable of covering short distances at great speed and a head full of tiny razor-sharp teeth.

IDENTITY

The pike is a near-perfect killing machine and the ultimate freshwater predator.

With its green and yellow polka dot markings, it is perfectly camouflaged and able to lurk in the underwater shadows waiting to strike. Couple that with a long, lean body capable of covering short distances at great speed and a head full of tiny razor-sharp teeth, and you have a creature perfectly suited to eating other fish. Pike are also blessed with very good eyesight and a good sense of smell – something that is vital if the water is coloured.

The biggest pike to be caught in British waters weighed in at 46lb 13oz and was taken by Roy Lewis from Llandegfedd Reservoir in 1992.

DISTRIBUTION

Pike are found throughout Great Britain. Apart from on heavily managed fisheries, pike will survive wherever there is fish for them to prey on.

LOCATION

Pike can be found in almost all venues where there is enough food for them to eat. Ponds, lakes and gravel pits all hold them, as do canals, drains and rivers, too. Knowing where to start fishing for pike can be difficult because they like to move around. But the normal features you would look for if perch were the target – bridges, underwater structures, holes in weed beds, overhanging trees and drop offs – are all worth investigating. Basically anywhere that provides an ambush point is a good place to start.

Of the two sexes, female pike grow much larger than males and 'jacks' will gather around the females at spawning time in order to try and fertilise the eggs.

DIET

As a predatory species, pike eat a diet predominantly consisting of fish. They don't seem to favour any particular type and prefer to make life easy for themselves by targeting those that are wounded or distressed. They are greedy,

too. Even small pike have been known to take on sizeable prey, with some even perishing as a result of biting off more than they can chew – literally! Fish are the mainstay of their diet, but they are sometimes supplemented by the likes of water rodents and ducklings. Pike are essentially opportunist feeders, so whatever comes easily will be consumed. Spawning time normally takes in spring when the water temperature reaches 48F (9C). Pike are regarded as a winter species, primarily because they are prepared to feed in all but the coldest weather.

TACTICS

The traditional – and most consistently successful – way of catching pike is with fish, either alive or dead. Popular coarse

baits are roach, rudd and skimmer bream, although sea fish like mackerel, herring and lamprey are very successful. Should you choose to livebait, ensure the fishery allows the practice. Also make sure you only use fish caught from the venue you are fishing – transferring live fish from one place to another is illegal. Fish baits are then presented on a leger or float rig but whatever you choose, ensure your tackle is up to the job. And remember, a wire trace is absolutely essential.

Aside from using fish as bait, another highly effective way of catching pike is with a lure. They are an instinctive species that can be triggered into feeding mode with a carefully worked spinner, plug or jig.

Whatever method you use for catching pike, be very careful when you have them on the bank. They might be the apex predator in your water, but they are extremely vulnerable when removed from their home. An unhooking mat and forceps are crucial pieces of kit. If in doubt, go pike fishing with someone with experience before going alone.

The Latin name for pike is esox luscious

Up until relatively recently, the pike was considered something of a delicacy in this country. Many cultures still eat pike but critics complain it has a muddy taste.

Be extremely careful when unhooking pike. Not only do they possess hundreds of very sharp teeth, their gill rakers are highly abrasive and will remove skin easily.

The biggest pike to be caught in British waters weighed in at 46lb 13oz and was taken by Roy Lewis from Llandegfedd Reservoir in 1992.

FIVE BAITS TO TRY FOR PIKE

ROACH LIVEBAIT
MACKEREL
SMELT
SPINNERS
PLUGS

ROACH...

You'll find roach in lakes, ponds, pits, canals, drains and rivers. Their favoured habitat are stillwaters and the lower reaches of rivers.

IDENTITY

Widespread throughout nearly every type of different venue, the roach is one of our most popular coarse fish.

Occasionally confused with rudd, the colouration of the roach is silver with a blue hue, whereas the rudd tends to be more golden. The roach has an orange eye and fins that are a vibrant red.

However, the one telling difference between the two species is the mouth. The roach has lips that are level; the rudd has a protruding bottom lip.

DISTRIBUTION

Perhaps the most common freshwater fish in Europe, the roach can be found throughout England.

LOCATION

You'll find roach in lakes, ponds, pits canals, drains and rivers. Their favoured habitat are stillwaters and the lower reaches of rivers where the pace of the flow is not too quick. They are a very hardy species and one that is known to survive where others perish when there has been a pollution.

One of the problems anglers can find is that, because of their durability, some venues will contain thousands of roach – but they'll all be small. Essentially the fish can't get any bigger because the food source is limited.

Spawning takes place in the shallows between April and June. The average female fish lays around 20,000 eggs per 1lb of body weight.

DIET

Roach like to feed on the bottom, rooting around for grubs like snails and insect larvae. Bloodworms, though, are perhaps the favourite 'natural' bait.

But although they are recognised as

ABOVE A typical sized roach

LEFT Roach might be widespread but bigger specimens are hard to find

RIGHT A superb bag of roach taken on pole tactics

preferring to feed on the deck, will come to surface in warm water to take surface insects and they will often reveal their presence to anglers by 'rolling.' Roach aren't a fish that grows to a huge size. Catch one over 1lb and you have a meritorious fish. The British record might stand at 4lb 4oz, but specimens close to this size – and even in the 3lb mark – are extremely rare.

TACTICS

Floatfishing – by running line or on the pole – is the best method of catching small roach. Hempseed, especially in winter and this is excellent to use as loosefeed. It will keep fish in the swim without filling them up. It can be used as hookbait but because of its tiny size it can be difficult to hook. Breadpunch is a great alternative, likewise maggots. If bigger roach are the target, and you want to fish a river, opt for a lump of breadflake over liquidised bread. If you're targeting stillwaters, then mini-boilies work well – especially on venues where carpers have introduced a lot of standard-sized boilies.

FACTFILE

The latin name for roach is rutilus rutilus.

Roach are the most widespread of coarse fish and our found in all types of venues.

They are a shoal fish, often moving in huge numbers.

Watch out for hybrids. Roach will regularly breed with rudd and bream and the offspring will have characteristics of both.

Lobworm is the staple natural diet of the roach.

FIVE BAITS TO TRY FOR ROACH

MAGGOTS
CASTERS
HEMP
BREADPUNCH
SWEETCORN

TENCH...

They feed almost exclusively on the bottom where they root around in the mud for worms, snails, mussels and bloodworm.

IDENTITY

One of our most recognisable of freshwater fish, the tench, with its distinctive green colouring, velvet-like skin and red eye, is impossible to confuse with anything else. A member of the carp family, it can range in colouration from almost black to a very pale green and an ornamental variety exists that is golden yellow in colour.

DISTRIBUTION

Throughout the UK and Europe, except northern Scotland, Iceland and Russia.

LOCATION

Tench are predominantly found in ponds, lakes and gravel pits, and while they do inhabit canals and rivers, they are much more suited to rich stillwaters where they can leisurely feed in silt and mud on the bottom.

Spawning doesn't take place until water temperatures have warmed after winter and that means they lay eggs later than most coarse fish.

Many specimen anglers catch the very biggest tench in May or June – just prior to the species spawning and some fish can weigh an extra 2lb to 3lb or more if caught when 'spawn-bound'. Each pair takes several weeks to spawn, leaving clusters of eggs stuck to the stems of water plants. Big females can carry close to one million eggs.

DIET

They feed almost exclusively on the bottom where they root around in the mud for worms, snails, mussels and bloodworm.

When they feed, they release tiny pockets of bubbles from their mouth, which can appear frothy when they break the water's surface.

Feeding times tend to be predominantly at dawn, although tench will feed through the day – especially so on gravel pits - with another hotspot at dusk.

LEFT Tench are synonymous with summer

ABOVE Tench love to feed in silt and mud on the bottom of lakes and ponds

RIGHT The distinctive green colouring of a tench is displayed brilliantly here

TACTICS

If you intend to fish a pond or lake, then a float can be the best approach. Tench are a species that love the margins and can often be caught just a rod length or two from the bank. Bait-wise, sweetcorn, maggots, casters, bread or small boilies will all catch.

However, if you are on a gravel pit, the fish tend to be further out making legering the best tactic. Here, use either a bomb or a swimfeeder to get that extra distance and small boilies tend to be most effective on the hook. Essentially, scaled-down carp tactics are the order of the day.

FACTFILE

The Latin name for tench is tinca tinca.

Known as the 'doctor fish', ancient legend says the slime which coats the body of the tench has healing properties.

Tench can be found in most lowland lakes, some slow moving rivers and canals.

The tench thrives best in very weedy waters with a rich, muddy bottom although they are very tolerant of stagnant conditions.

The average tench lives up to 10-15 years of age.

FIVE BAITS TO TRY FOR TENCH

SWEETCORN
MAGGOTS
BREAD
CASTERS
BOILIES

CATFISH AND CRUCIAN CARP...

There are numerous other freshwater species that live in the British Isles and although they might not be as widespread – or as popular – as those already detailed, they are worth noting.

CATFISH

The wels catfish is unmistakeable and resembles no other species. With their huge heads, tiny eyes, long whiskers, small dorsal fins and tadpole-like bodies, they are completely unique in appearance. UK catfish can be found in selected stillwater venues. They are largely bottom feeders but have been known to take prey near the surface, especially as night falls.

As a nocturnal species, catfish usually spend daylight hours hidden amongst tree roots and weed beds. Catfish are a predatory fish and are not fussy in the slightest. Live, dying or decaying fish will all be eaten, as will waterfowl, rodents and frogs. If catfish are the target then legering has to be the most

effective approach. They are a hard-fighting species and with fish up to 60lb possible on some venues, you'll need beefy carp rods, big pit reels and plenty of tough-as-old-boots line. Specially forged catfish hooks are advisable, such is the power of the fish. Bait-wise, live and dead coarse fish will work, as will huge fishmeal pellets, giant boilies and even bunches of worms.

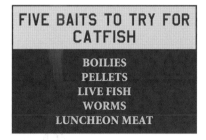

FIVE BAITS TO TRY FOR CATFISH

BOILIES
PELLETS
LIVE FISH
WORMS
LUNCHEON MEAT

CRUCIAN CARP

Although part of the carp family, the crucian carp is vastly different from commons, leathers or mirrors. Not only does its mouth not contain any barbules but it is also much smaller in size and rarely exceeds 4lb in weight.

Crucian carp love small, weedy ponds where they love to forage for food on the bottom and will routinely eat bloodworm, midge larvae and snails. Floatfishing is the best way of catching crucians. They are known as shy-biting fish so a finely-shotted float, with just a few millimetres showing above the surface, is ideal, with bread, sweetcorn or maggots the best bait.

FIVE BAITS TO TRY FOR CRUCIAN CARP

BREAD
MAGGOTS
CASTERS
SWEETCORN
PELLETS

ABOVE Unlike their larger family members, crucian carp rarely exceed 4lb

LEFT catfish can grow extremely large like this monster!

DACE AND EELS...

DACE

The dace is a small fish rarely exceeding 1lb. They have yellow eyes, a dark grey dorsal fin, with yellow/orange anal and pelvic fins. They are sometimes confused with small chub but an instant check can be done to alleviate any confusion. The dorsal fin is concave (bends inwards) whereas on a chub it is convex (bends outwards).

Dace prefer clean, fast-flowing rivers and streams with gravel beds. They move around in huge shoals that can often be thousands strong. Their natural diet includes shrimp, algae, floating insects and small snails.

Floatfishing for dace is the most effective way of catching them. Trotted maggots work best, with a little-and-often approach to feeding the best way to go.

FIVE BAITS FOR DACE

MAGGOT
CASTER
BREADPUNCH
HEMP
REDWORM

EELS

Long and lean, the freshwater eel is unmistakable in its appearance. With olive brown flanks and deeply-buried scales, it's smooth to the the touch and extremely difficult to handle. It has a long dorsal fin, two tiny pectoral fins and can grow to weights in excess of 8lb.

The life-cycle of the eel is remarkable. Born in the Sargasso Sea, they our coastline as tiny elvers before moving up river systems and into lakes, ponds and canals. They have been known to cross land in order to reach water.

As adults they attempt to return to the Sargasso, but many remain 'land-locked' and are unable to escape. These fish tend to grow the biggest. Eels are largely a nocturnal feeder and love to scavenge on dead and dying fish. They will also eat the corpses of any other animal matter, as well as invertebrates. If you want to target eels, night fishing is best. Try legering a bunch of worms, or a small dead roach, for the best results.

ABOVE An eel lies in ambush

LEFT Floatfishing with maggots in fast-flowing rivers is a great combination to catch dace like this

FIVE BAITS FOR EELS

LOBWORM
RAOCH DEADBAIT
DEAD MAGGOTS
STRIPS OF STEAK
FISHMEAL BOILIE

RUDD AND ZANDER...

RUDD

Not to be mistaken for roach, rudd are a beautiful fish that are golden in appearance and boast brilliant blood-red fins. Along with colouration, another way to tell rudd from roach is by studying the mouth. The rudd has an angled bottom lip that protrudes, whereas the mouth of the roach is level. The rudd's dorsal fin is also set back and it has a much deeper body than the roach. Once widespread across the UK, hybridisation with roach, the dominance of carp and general habitat destruction have led to the demise of the rudd. Pockets still exist and the deep, clear gravel pits of East Anglia are still home to the species, as are the drains and rivers in that area, too.

Rudd prefer stillwater venues and are rarely found in any great numbers in rivers. Deep, weedy and clear gravel pits provide a superb environment for rudd to survive, as do slow-moving and overgrown drains and canals. The rudd is a surface feeder and in warm weather they love to cruise in the top layers

BELOW The beautiful golden colurings of a rudd

of water eating insects. However, they will also eat bloodworm and bottom-dwelling crustaceans. If rudd are the target floatfishing provides the best way of catching them. 'Up-in-the-water' tactics can be extremely effective and this can be achieved by constantly spraying maggots to draw the fish into the top layers and get them competing for food.

FIVE BAITS FOR RUDD

MAGGOTS
CASTERS
SWEETCORN
BREADFLAKE,
MINI BOILIES

ZANDER

The zander is a much-maligned species that has been wrongly accused in the past for the decreasing numbers of silverfish. It has a light olive-brown back with grey bars down its flanks and two dorsal fins – the first of which is long and spined. The zander also has a large head full of tiny, razor sharp teeth and eyes that often appear opaque. This is because it has adapted to feed in murky water. They are not a widespread species but are happy to live in lakes, rivers and especially slow-moving drains. As predators, zander feed on other species like roach and skimmers. Most zander are caught on either floatfished or legered deadbaits. Like the perch, they don't like any form of resistance so any rigs need to be free-running. They have a particular preference for small coarse fish deadbaits, no bigger than three or four inches in length, with roach, rudd and skimmer bream ideal.

ABOVE Zander have large heads full of tiny, razor sharp teeth

FIVE BAITS FOR ZANDER

LAMPREY SECTION
HALF A ROACH DEADBAIT
JIGS
SHORT-BODIED PLUG
SMALL LIVEBAIT

CHAPTER 4

SKILLS SCHOOL

HOW TO
SPOOL A REEL...

> 66 *Match-type reels take around 100 metres of light 2lb to 3lb line.* 99

One common mistake many anglers make is incorrectly spooling their reel. Not only will this badly hinder casting, it will hamper retrieval and get in the way of playing fish correctly.

Line will need replacing at least once a season, and possibly more, depending on how much it used. Stress of constant casting, sunlight and abrasive underwater snags all weaken line – and weakened line can cost fish. Therefore, it's important to regularly check for signs of wear and tear.

Let's take a look at how spool a reel with this step-by-step guide...

1. First off, remove the spool from your reel and fix the reel body to the butt section of your rod.

2. Pass the spool of line through the ring or rings on the butt section of the rod and tie the loose end to the detached reel spool, using a simple double knot. Make sure this knot is situated at the bottom of the spool and not in the middle where it could hinder casting.

3. Once this is secure, open the bail arm on your reel and put the spool back on. Then close the bail arm and you will be ready to start winding.

4. To do this, take a bucket of water and drop the spool of line into this and start winding. By being in the water the line will be kept continually tight, making for decent line lay and stopping any chance of tangles or loose coils of line that will affect casting.

ABOVE A correctly spooled reel

LINE CAPACITY

Almost every reel you look at will have a line capacity on the side of the spool. This tells you roughly how much line of a certain breaking strain or diameter will be needed to fill the reel spool neatly up to the lip. Match-type reels take around 100 metres of light 2lb to 3lb line, whereas reels designed for bigger fish like carp and pike will take a lot more line, sometimes up to 300m of 10lb mono.

BACKING

If you don't want to wind the capacity of line onto your reel, you can use 'backing' to help bulk the spool out. This comes in many forms but a popular one is electrician's tape wrapped round the spool until it is half full. Line can then be wound on over this.

HOW TO
CAST...

" *The most important thing to master is judging when to let go of the trapped line.* **"**

Casting is perhaps the most important skill to be mastered because if you can't do it correctly, the chances of catching fish is virtually nil.

Let's take a look at how to perfect it with this step-by-step guide...

1. Ensure you have the right amount of line between rod tip and float or feeder. This will make the casting process a lot smoother. If the line is too short the cast becomes jerky and will often not reach the intended destination, tangling on the way. Around 3ft of line is ample in most situations.

2. With the rod placed in a straight line directly behind you, the butt facing out into your swim, hold the rod over your shoulder parallel to the ground with the float or swimfeeder hanging but not touching the ground.

3. Hold the rod around the reel seat with one hand, trapping the line coming off the reel against the rod butt using your forefinger.

4. With your other hand undo the bail arm. Then grip the base of the rod handle with this hand.

5. Sweep the rod upwards from its position and follow it through until the tip is pointing out into the lake. As you do this, release the line trapped by your finger, roughly when the rod is pointing vertically upwards.

6. The compression built up by the rod through the cast will provide enough power and spring in the top sections of the rod to launch the float or swim-feeder to its destination.

7. The most important thing to master is judging when to let go of the trapped line. Too early and the line will spill off the spool at the wrong time, too late and the cast will be too short.

BELOW Once you've mastered how to cast you'll have a much better chance of catching fish

HOW TO
SHOT A FLOAT...

If the float sinks, you are too shallow but if it lies flat on the surface, you are too deep.

BELOW Large shot

RIGHT Crystal wagglers in various sizes

Floatfishing is one of the most pleasurable forms of fishing but your float must be set-up correctly in order to get the most from it.

The shotting is key. Too much weight and the float will sink and become useless, whereas not enough shot will leave too much of the float's tip above water and bite detection will become impossible.

The ideal way to shot a float is to have just a few millimetres showing – this way any bite will result in the tip disappearing and this is a signal to strike.

SO WHERE DO I PUT THE SHOT?

Modern floats carry graphics indicating how much shot is required for it to sit correctly in the water. A basic float rig should have the bulk of the shot 'locked' either side of the float, with smaller shot placed further down the line depending on what species are the target.

When aiming to catch small fish such as roach and rudd, spread the shot out so you get a slow fall of the bait through the water. These are species often feed off the bottom and can be caught what is known as 'on the drop.'

For bottom-feeding species such as bream and tench, it's better to have these shot placed together or bulked, at around two-thirds of the way down the line. This means your bait sinks to the bottom immediately, missing out any small fish feeding off the bottom.

FIND THE RIGHT DEPTH

Finding the depth when floatfishing is essential because different species feed at different depths. Simply set up your rig with an estimated depth and attach a plummet to the hook. If the float sinks, you are too shallow but if it lies flat on the surface, you are too deep. Keep adjusting the depth until you have found the correct depth.

WHAT FLOAT TO USE?

Floats generally come in two types - those that are attached through an eye, known as wagglers, and those attached via rubbers, known as stick floats. Stick floats are exclusively used on rivers and wagglers are commonly used on stillwaters.

INSERT WAGGLERS

These are used on lakes, canals and slow-flowing rivers where there's less chance of the flow pulling the float under. They have plastic or balsa wood body with a thinner piece of plastic or wood at the tip.

BODIED WAGGLER

As the name suggests, these floats have a large body at their base with a balsa wood stem and tip. These are used for casting long distances on big rivers and lakes.

CRYSTAL WAGGLER

Made from clear plastic, with a bright coloured tip, these types of floats have the advantage of being invisible to fish. They come in straight or insert styles.

STICK FLOATS

These floats are not attached by the bottom end, instead being held on the line by three silicone float rubbers at the top, middle and bottom of the float and are commonly used on rivers for trotting through the swim.

HOW TO SET UP A LEGER RIG...

 Being aerodynamically shaped a bomb will cast a long way, even in strong winds.

Legering is a tactic that is used when floatfishing becomes impossible. For example, the wind maybe too strong for a float to be presented correctly, the fish could at long range or the target species (like carp) may require a night fishing approach that renders a float useless.

There are two types of legering – either with a bomb or with a swimfeeder.

The bomb is basically a pear-shaped lead weight that can be cast a distance, whereas the swimfeeder carries bait that ensures there are some free offerings near your hookbait.

Let's have a look at the different types of bombs and swimfeeders....

BOMB

These are quite simply a pear-shaped lead with a swivel folded into the top that allows the line to be attached. Being aerodynamically shaped a bomb will cast a long way, even in strong winds. They come in a variety of sizes.

WATCH LEAD

Borrowed from sea fishing, these are

ideal in flooded river conditions when barbel are the target. They feature grips and these hold bottom in fast water conditions.

LINK LEGER

A link leger is simply shot pinched onto a piece of line coming off the main line. Typical shots range between BB and SSGs. Ideal in clear water conditions when chub or roach are target.

BLOCKEND FEEDER

Used for carrying loose offerings or particles such as maggots, casters, hempseed and pellets, the blockend feeder, is capped off at each end to hold the feed in. It also features a lead strip to give it casting weight and is ideal for chub, barbel or roach.

GROUNDBAIT FEEDER

The groundbait feeder is a plastic tube with holes, attached to a strip of lead,

ABOVE A selection of leger weights

that isn't capped at either end. Before casting the feeder is plugged with groundbait at each end, allowing the middle section to be filled with the likes of maggots or casters.

METHOD FEEDER

The method is a weighted plastic frame that is designed to be used with a stiff groundbait moulded around it, creating a 'method ball'. This is fished with a short hooklength, mainly for carp.

HOW TO
USE A POLE...

> *Unlike with rod and line, striking at a bite doesn't require anything more than a sharp lift of the pole.*

Pole fishing has become one of the most effective ways of catching fish and is the preferred tactic of the match angler. The pole provides excellent presentation – and this can often provide vital extra bites when the going gets tough.

Made of a series of sections, poles can be anything from a few metres in length to anything up to 18 metres.

Here are five reasons why the pole is such a superb method...

I. FANTASTIC PRESENTATION

The pole also offers angler supreme accuracy and presentation because you have the pole tip directly above your float and there's very little line for the wind to get hold of. Also, if you miss a bite it is simply a matter of lifting the rig out of the water and dropping it back in to get fishing again. Feeding is also straightforward. Simply attach a pole cup and drop the bait – whether it be groundbait or loosefeed – over the top.

2. STRIKING MADE EASY

Unlike with rod and line, striking at a bite doesn't require anything more than a sharp lift of the pole. Because you are directly above the float, you only need minimal power to set the hook.

3. LET THE ELASTIC TAKE THE STRAIN

To land fish on the pole you must use a length of internal elastic that runs through the top sections. These elastics come in various strengths depending on the size of fish you are after with No 1 the lightest available up to a whopping No 20. This elastic acts as a buffer and prevents the line breaking, while at the same time tiring the fish out.

4. FINESSE WITH FLOATS

Standard floats, like wagglers and sticks, aren't designed for use with the pole and there are purpose-made floats for the job. These tend to be much smaller and delicate, largely because they are lowered into the water rather than cast out. They are attached via an eye on the side of the float and a float rubber on the thin wire stem at their base.

5. PLAYING RULES

Once you've struck at a bite and connected with a fish, keep the pole low and parallel to the water. Once the fish has stopped running you can begin unshipping using a pole roller. Gently edge the pole back behind you, ensuring you keep a tight line to the fish at all times. When you have unshipped fully, break the pole down, still keeping that tight line. Then slowly lift the top sections of the unshipped pole into an upright position, much as you would a rod. This will bring the fish up to the surface. If the fish runs, drop the pole back parallel with water and wait for it to finish.

LEFT Poles allow for perfect presentation

HOW TO
TIE BASIC KNOTS...

" Water knot – used for constructing a paternoster
link when legering with a bomb or swimfeeder. "

Knots are absolutely vital to your set up and a handful must be mastered before you can fish effectively.

Here are three that will cater for almost all eventualities...

HALF☐TUCKED BLOOD KNOT

Used for eyed hooks and swivels

1. Pass the line through the eye of the hook (or swivel) and bring it back on itself so the line lays side by side.

2. Take the loose end and twist this around the mainline between five and seven times. Make sure the mainline is held tight at all times.

3. Take the loose end and pass this through the little loop created between the hook or swivel and the first twist in the line.

4. Pull the loose end, moistening the knot with saliva to prevent line damage. You may also need to push the knot together once it has been tightened to make it tidy. Trim the tag end leaving enough to compensate for any slippage during use.

OVERHAND LOOP

Used for creating loops to attach hook-lengths

1. Double the line back on itself, creating a looped end.

2. Hold this looped end and pass it back on itself and then over the doubled up line below.

3. Pass the end twice through the loop you've just created.

4. Pull the end tightly until the knot is secure and line tight. Trim the tag end.

WATER KNOT

Used for constructing a paternoster link when legering with a bomb or swimfeeder.

1. Place your hooklength material (normally between two feet and a few inches) alongside your mainline.

2. Make a loop and carefully thread the

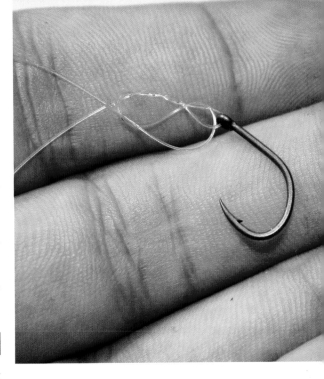

two lines through the loop four times.

3. Moisten and pull tight.

4. The 'tail' from the mainline should be used to tie on the swimfeeder or bomb while a hook should be attached to the hooklength line.

ABOVE Tying the correct knot decreases the chances of line breaks

HOW TO
MIX GROUNDBAIT...

> 66 *Once you think the mix has enough water, stop adding liquid and with both hands, thoroughly mix the groundbait...* 99

Groundbait is the perfect way of enticing – and keeping – fish in your swim. It is especially effective when targeting shoal fish like bream and roach, as well as bigger species like carp and tench.

So what is groundbait? Essentially, it's ground down products such as biscuits, breadcrumbs, seeds and nuts that, when mixed with water, can be moulded into balls for throwing into your swim by hand or feeding via a swimfeeder.

However, mixing it correctly requires skill because if you add too much water, you could be left with an unusable,

stodgy mess that the fish won't like the look of one bit.

Here's how to mix it correctly...

1. Pour the dry groundbait into a large, round-sided bowl or bucket. If you intend to use more than one variety of groundbait, add both of these and mix them thoroughly by hand to ensure they are evenly distributed.

2. Take a small bowl of water (use water from the venue you are fishing) and create a small well in the middle of the dry crumb. Slowly pour water into this well a little at a time, agitating the groundbait while pouring to ensure the liquid is well distributed and there are no wetter or dryer areas.

3. Once you think the mix has enough water, stop adding liquid and with both hands, thoroughly mix the groundbait to disperse any wet patches you haven't found. Leave the mix to stand for a few minutes to ensure all water has been absorbed.

4. Check to see if any additional water is needed. Ideally, you should be able to form a ball with one squeeze but when you rub it between your hands it should fall apart easily.

5. Once ready, place a maggot riddle over another bucket and pour the mixed contents onto the riddle and sieve the mix through into the empty bucket. This will remove any larger lumps or particles that would otherwise fill the fish up, especially important in winter where the fish will only want small amounts of bait. What you should be left with is a fine mixture that makes a ball easily but breaks apart just as simply.

6. It's at this point that you should add any maggots, casters, sweetcorn or hemp.

CHAPTER 5

FISH HABITAT

FINDING FISH
ON A CANAL...

66 *Look to the far bank, where there is often cover, to find chub and carp.* 99

Canals were originally dug to allow barges to transport goods from one city to another in the 1700s. With this purpose long since redundant, nowadays they are mostly used for leisure pursuits like boating – and fishing.

There are numerous canals across the UK, many of which run for miles and miles, and nearly all hold a good head of coarse fish.

Certain areas on canals are better than others, with old boat-turning bays, marinas and bridges all obvious holding spots, but expect to find fish throughout entire stretches.

A UNIFORM SHAPE

The most common species found in canals are roach, rudd, bream, tench, perch, pike, carp and chub.

Fish don't grow as big in canals as they do in lakes and rivers, largely down to the amount of food available, but they still provide the angler with a unique challenge.

Nearly all canals have a uniform shape – a throwback to their original design for allowing boats, or barges, to transport goods. Therefore, it is easier to predict where the various species live.

Roach, rudd, bream and perch will be found down the central track of the canal, where they congregate in big shoals.

Look to the far bank, where there is often cover, to find chub and carp, while pike will often be found lurking in the nearside margins where they wait in pursuit of prey.

ABOVE A good example of cover on the far bank where chub and carp may be hiding

ABOVE Nearly all canals have a uniform shape for boats and barges

far bank. The bottom of these venues tend to be rich in life, with bloodworm predominant. Another staple diet of the fish will be beetles, leeches and snails.

HOW DO I TACKLE IT?

Floatfishing is generally considered the best way of getting the most from a canal, with many anglers preferring to pole fish.

Poles have the ability to reach the far bank on most of these venues and their near perfect presentation means they are a great success.

Roach, rudd, perch, bream and tench can all be caught on the pole but if you want to target the carp or pike, a specialist approach with rod and line is advisable.

TRY THE OPPOSITE BANK

Most canals have at least one towpath running alongside them for walkers and cyclists. However, more often than not, the far bank will be inaccessible and overgrown – providing the angler with a perfect area to target.

If the canal is still used frequently by leisure boaters, weed growth in the central track is likely to be minimal, with most of the pondweed and milfoil found in the margins both on the near and

WHAT CAN I CATCH?

ROACH, RUDD, BREAM, TENCH, CARP, PIKE , PERCH

FINDING FISH
ON A LAKE...

66 *Most established lakes and ponds will be surrounded by overhanging trees – this is where carp can be found.* 99

While some lakes are completely natural, having found existence thanks to ancient land shift, many are the result of agricultural practice.

Land belonging to farmers is littered with ponds and lakes, originally built to water livestock or for irrigation, which now have become a haven for coarse fish.

Many of these waters, most of which are more than 50 years old, are now used for a second purpose – angling.

LEFT Mature lakes are home to a variety of coarse fish species

A VARIETY OF SPECIES

The common species in lakes and ponds include roach, rudd, tench, bream, carp, pike and perch.

Roach and rudd will generally be found in great numbers but as a consequence are unlikely to reach specimen size. However, in abundance they are generally easy to catch.

Tench and bream will feed over silt beds and give themselves away by blowing feeding bubbles to the surface. Most established lakes and ponds will be surrounded by overhanging trees – this is where carp can be found.

The type of predators to be found in such a water are pike and perch. Both love to find shady areas where they can wait in ambush for small fish.

A RICH ENVIRONMENT

Due to their age, these lakes and ponds tend to be well established – not just by fish – but also by all manner of wildlife, both above and below the water's surface. As such, they can be thoroughly enjoyable places to fish.

The bottom of these venues tends to be rich in bloodworms and larvae, while water beetles, leeches, snails and water boatmen give the fish plenty to feed on. Such a rich environment ensures weed growth is prolific, with milfoil, hornwort and all manner of pondweed prevalent. Expect to see lily pads and reed mace too.

HOW DO I TACKLE IT?

Lakes can be fished in a variety of different ways. You can floatfish with a rod or pole for roach, rudd and perch, or use a feeder to catch bream. Carp and tench can also be caught from lakes on standard leger tactics.

Most lakes and ponds tend to have a uniform shape, shelving gently down the margins to depths between six and eight feet. They also tend to be mature, surrounded by trees and vegetation and with heavy weed growth.

WHAT CAN I CATCH?

ROACH, RUDD, TENCH, BREAM, CARP, PIKE, PERCH

FINDING FISH
ON A GRAVEL PIT...

66 *Facing a large expanse of water can be a daunting
prospect but don't be put off by the size.* **99**

**Unlike lakes and ponds, many of which
are either natural or well-established,
gravel pits are a relatively modern
occurrence.**

Over the last 50 years the UK has
undergone major changes, with both
the boom in housing and the need for
better road links inadvertently providing anglers with some brilliant fishing.
The demand for houses and motorways
saw gravel workings spring up all across
the country, with material needed in
vast amounts for construction work.

Once this material had been removed

from the ground, huge holes were left
that eventually filled with water and
now, with many reaching maturity,
provide superb fishing.

UNPREDICTABLE DEPTH

All fish species can be found in gravel
pits, with roach, rudd, bream, tench,
carp, pike, perch and catfish the most
common. Location on huge expanses of
water can often be the biggest problem to
overcome, but by spending time learning
and studying the water you can formu-
late some idea of what lives where.

Due to their original purpose of providing gravel the bottom of these pits tend to be extremely uneven and unpredictable. They can be as much as 20 feet deep in one place, yet yards away they can be extremely shallow. They also tend to boast lots of islands too.

FINDING THE FISH

Coarse fish are creatures of habit and will have similar characteristics to those that live in other still water like ponds, lakes and canals – but in fewer numbers. Tench, carp and catfish can be found in the margins, roach and rudd will shoal but in fewer numbers, while bream will be in the deeper areas of the pit. As predators, perch and pike will hunt close to where the food fish are.

Weed growth is often prolific, with pondweed the most predominant and thick on many pits. However, suitable spawning areas are few and far between on pits, so fish tend to be lower in numbers. But with less competition for food, they are bigger in size.

HOW DO I TACKLE IT?

Facing a large expanse of water can be a daunting prospect but don't be put off by the size. One of the real keys to success is finding what depth the water is in front of you and where the clear areas are. This isn't as hard as it sounds.

Try casting a lead weight – on of around one ounce is about right – into different areas of the swim. Count the number of seconds it takes to hit the bottom (one second roughly equates to one foot) to establish depth and then gently reel in to determine the make up of the bottom.

If you are struggling to reel in, you're in weed, whereas if it comes in freely, you have found a clear area. It's here you should base your attack.

WHAT CAN I CATCH?

ROACH, RUDD, TENCH, BREAM, CARP, PIKE, PERCH, CATFISH

FINDING FISH
ON A RIVER...

" Rivers can be difficult to 'read' but there are several hotspots that will almost certainly contain fish... "

Rivers provide some of the best fishing there is to be had – but they require a different approach to those used when stillwater angling.

As entirely naturally entities, rivers can be unpredictable and many change appearance from one day to the next.

Rivers can come in all shapes and sizes, varying from small, fast, shallow streams no more than a few yards wide, to huge, deep, wide and sluggish waterways. But one thing remains consistent – they all contain fish.

FULL OF LIFE

All rivers start in the same place – on high ground where they begin life as a stream. But these streams grow up and as they wind themselves through hills and mountains many grow into big rivers up to 50 metres wide.

Rivers are generally full of life – both under the water and above it.

All fish species inhabit rivers with chub, barbel, dace and roach among the most popular species. On the bottom, in among the gravel, sand and silt ranunculus, bulrushes and reedmace grow in abundance.

The generally high quality of the water in rivers means that water lice, midge larvae, snails, bloodworm, mussels and crayfish thrive in many river venues providing the resident species with a huge natural larder.

FINDING THE FISH

Rivers can be difficult to 'read' but there are several hotspots that will almost certainly contain fish.

Well oxygenated water, especially in warmer months, is where the fish like to congregate so look for slightly deeper holes at the end of fast runs. Fish will be waiting for food to be carried down into the current.

Fish love the cover of weed and will cruise in an out in search of food so look for clear areas, particularly those containing gravel, because many river fish like to feed over a hard bottom.

Undercut banks, overhanging trees and reed beds are also obvious holding areas, with barbel, chub, perch, roach, bream, dace, pike and grayling the most likely species to be found in running water.

HOW DO I TACKLE IT?

There are two basic ways of tackling a typical middle river swim – with a simple leger set-up or with float.

Legering is probably the most effective way of catching barbel and chub, whereas the float will be more successful if roach and dace are the target.

Be prepared to be mobile, wandering from swim to swim until you find the fish. Often you will catch only a few fish before you need to move on.

A basic paternoster set-up with either luncheon meat, bread or worm will account for chub and barbel, whereas maggots, casters or punch will be most effective for roach, dace or grayling.

WHAT CAN I CATCH?

ROACH, CHUB, BARBEL, BREAM, PERCH, ROACH, PIKE, GRAYLING, DACE

FINDING FISH
ON A WEIR POOL...

*" If you want to catch barbel or chub,
look for the fast water and tackle up accordingly. "*

Weir pools are a magnet for a whole host of different species and really come into their own during the summer months.

Built across rivers to either raise the upstream water level or control downstream flow, the water that tumbles over the weir mixes with air as it falls and so becomes well oxygenated.

In hot weather, when oxygen levels on the rest of the river are low, weir pools become even more attractive to fish and become brilliant areas for the angler to target.

FAST WATER

The real beauty of weir pools is their design. Not only do they boast fast water, they also contain deep slacks, back eddies, slower water, and shallows – basically nearly all the differing river environments in one place. As such, they are home to lots of different species. Barbel, chub, perch, roach, bream, perch and pike will all be found within the vicinity of a weir pool, each preferring its own particular area.Another superb feature of most weir pools is that they are often deeply undercut. This means that the concrete of the base of the weir protrudes several feet, providing superb cover underneath for species like barbel and chub.

FINDING FISH

Barbel and chub can be found in the very fast water that immediately falls over the weir or even beneath the sill. Both species love oxygenated water and in summer this is exactly where to find them. Species like bream, tench, roach and even carp, however, prefer a much more sedate pace and will congregate at the tail of the pool or in the deeper, slower moving slacks out of the direct flow. Pike and perch are never far away either, often sitting just out of the main flow where they wait to strike at prey.

HOW DO I TACKLE IT?

If you want to catch barbel or chub, look for the fast water and tackle up accordingly. Both fight hard in the fast flow so you'll need stout tackle. Remember that the river bed in weir pools is likely to be littered with all manner of debris brought

ABOVE Fishing a weir pool

down from upstream. It's one of the reasons fish are attracted to them. Heavy leads will also be needed to hold bottom in the current, so float fishing is not an option. In the slower water and slacks, a feeder and quivertip rod will best. Here you will most likely find the bream and tench. If you do want to floatfish, try trotting maggots at the tail of the weir pool were the bottom tends to be more uniform and the flow not so turbulent.

WHAT CAN I CATCH?

BARBEL, CHUB, BREAM, ROACH, TENCH, CARP, PIKE, PERCH

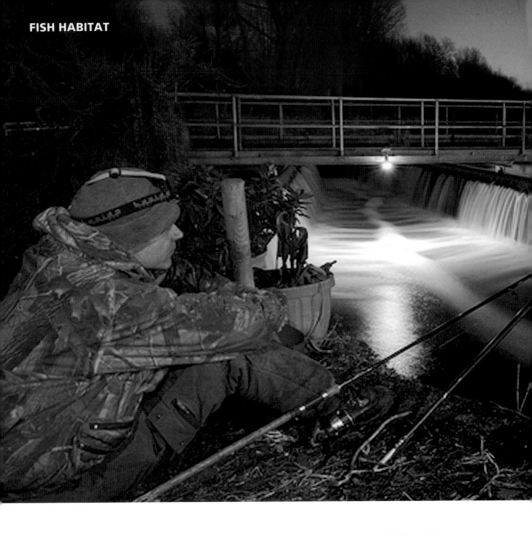

Night fishing on a weir pool

The pictures in this book were provided courtesy of the following:

STRIKE-ONE MEDIA, MATT HAYES, WIKIMEDIA COMMONS

Design & Artwork: ALEX YOUNG

Published by: DEMAND MEDIA LIMITED

Publisher: JASON FENWICK

Written by: MATT HAYES